Reading words
4–5

Author: Stephanie Cooper
Illustrator: Jacqui Bignell

How to use this book

Look out for these features!

IN THE ACTIVITIES

The parents' notes at the top of each activity will give you:
► a simple explanation about what your child is learning
► an idea of how you can work with your child on the activity.

This small page number guides you to the back of the book, where you will find further ideas for help.

AT THE BACK OF THE BOOK

Every activity has a section for parents containing:
► further explanations about what the activity teaches
► games that can be easily recreated at home
► questions to ask your child to encourage their learning
► tips on varying the activity if it seems too easy or too difficult for your child.

You will also find the answers at the back of the book.

HELPING YOUR CHILD AS THEY USE THIS BOOK

Why not try starting at the beginning of the book and work through it? Your child should only attempt one activity at a time. Remember, it is best to learn little and often when we are feeling wide awake!

EQUIPMENT YOUR CHILD WILL NEED

► a pencil for writing
► an eraser for correcting mistakes
► coloured pencils for drawing and colouring in.

You might also like to have ready some spare paper and some collections of objects (for instance, small toys, Lego bricks, buttons...) for some of the activities.

Contents

Match the words

Match the words. Join them with a line.

the

yes

me

she

we

you

an

they

4

This activity will help your child to read these words even when they are not in a sentence.

Look carefully at the words and talk about how many letters each one has.

you
she
me
we
the
they
an
yes

More match the words

Now match these words.

look

go

of

for

going

to

no

on

► Learning these common words will help with independent reading and writing.

► Talk about the shape of the words – how each has the letter 'o', and how they look similar.

going

for

no

look

go

on

to

of

You, I, or we?

Choose either **you**, **I** or **we** to go with each picture.

1. ___ are at school.

2. __ am reading.

► This activity will help your child learn how to read 'you', 'I' and 'we'.

► Ask your child questions such as "Where are the children? Do you think the words say 'I am at school' or 'we are at school'?"

Parents

42

3. _ _ _ _ are a clown.

4. _ am late.

5. _ _ _ _ are wet.

He or she?

Write in the missing words using **he** or **she**.

1. ___ runs.

2. ___ walks.

3. ____ jumps.

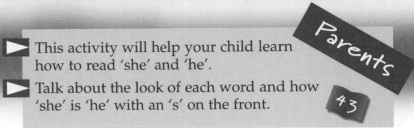

4. __ __ plays.

5. __ __ __ hops.

6. __ __ __ skips.

11

Yes or no?

Can you answer these questions using **yes** or **no**?

1. Do lions roar? _ _ _ _.

2. Are elephants big? _ _ _ _.

3. Do cats bark? _ _ _.

12

► This page will teach your child how to read the words 'yes' and 'no'.

► Read the questions aloud and ask your child to write 'yes' or 'no'.

Parents

43

4. Are clowns funny? _____.

5. Are apples orange? ____.

6. Can pigs fly? ____.

Woof woof!

Well-known words

Can you guess what Emma has been given for her birthday?
Read the words to help you decide.

| car | train | ball | scissors | teddy bear |
| computer | duck | umbrella | book |

1._____

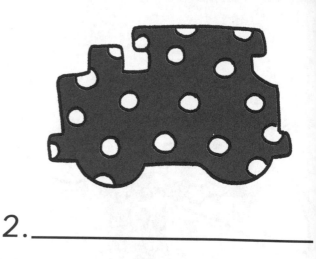

2._____

3._____

4._____

This activity will help your child to read some familiar words.

Ask them to look at the pictures and name each object before writing the appropriate words.

happy birthday emma

5._____

6._____

7._____

happy bir happy birthday h happy birthday happ appy birthday happ py bir thday happ

8._____

9._____

Missing words

Where is Abdul going? Choose the correct words from the box to finish each sentence.

1. Abdul is going to the _____.

2. Abdul is going to the _____.

► This activity will help your child choose words sensibly.

► Let your child choose words from the box to put at the end of each sentence. Do they make sense?

Parents

44

park   pond   ice cream van   swings

3. Abdul is going to the _____.

4. Abdul is going to the _____.

Lists

Finish this list.

I went to the shop to buy:

bananas

_____

_____

_____

_____

_____

_____

jam

sausages

apples

beans

Beans

tomato

Read a recipe

Tommy Toast is making a snack. Read his recipe.

Ingredients:

ham   cheese   bread

1. Toast the bread.

2. Put the ham and cheese onto the toast.

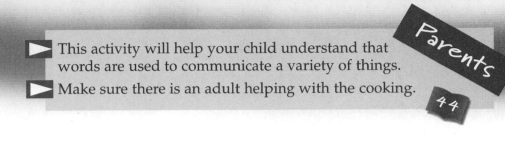

▶ This activity will help your child understand that words are used to communicate a variety of things.

▶ Make sure there is an adult helping with the cooking.

Parents

44

3. Grill it.

4. Eat it.

Now try to make your own toast,
with your parents' help.

Look at a letter

Read this letter from Jill.

Hello,
    Jack hurt his head when he fell down the hill.
    We dropped the bucket, too. Have you ever fallen over?

Love from Jill X

crown

pail

▶ This activity will help your child understand that words are used to communicate a variety of ideas.

Jack and Jill
Went up the hill,
To fetch a pail* of water;
Jack fell down,
And broke his crown**,
And Jill came tumbling after.

* **bucket**
** **head**

Dear Jill

Now write a letter back to Jill.
Tell her if you have ever fallen over.

Study a story

Nat has lots of pets and today he is washing them. Use the words in the box to finish the sentences.

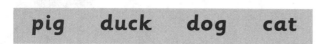

pig   duck   dog   cat

1. In goes the

_____.

Splish, splash.

2. In goes the

_____.

Splish, _____.

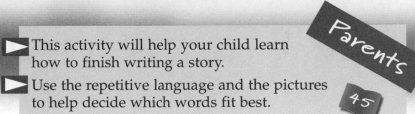

This activity will help your child learn how to finish writing a story.

Use the repetitive language and the pictures to help decide which words fit best.

Parents

45

3. In goes the

_____.

S_____ , _____.

4. In goes the

_____.

_____ , _____.

Now draw and write your own story.

_____

_____

_____.

25

The Enormous Turnip

Choose a word from the box
to fill in the missing words.

| dog | cat |
| rat | frog |

1. The man pulls
the turnip.

2. The man and
the ＿＿＿ pull the turnip.

3. The man, the ＿＿＿ and
the ＿＿＿＿ pull the turnip.

This activity will show your child how to use pictures to help read a story.

Use the pictures as a clue to find the missing words.

4. The man, the ___ ___, the ___ ___ ___ and the ___ ___ pull the turnip.

5. The man, the dog, the ___ ___ ___, the cat and the ___ ___ pull the turnip.

6. They all pull the turnip out!

Now copy the sentences on a clean piece of paper.

Reading rhyme words

Look for things in this picture that rhyme.
Write a list here.

cat   mat   Pat
    dog   log
            wig
goat
        Roy
            Stan
mouse
            bell

This activity will help your child to understand rhyming words.

Talk about the picture first, then the words, and name the animals and objects.

Stan

deep well

Funky Fox goes surfing

Read the sentences. Choose the best one to go with each picture and write it out.

Funky Fox went to the sea.

He took his shoes off.

► This activity will help your child make sense of a story.
► Introduce the name Funky Fox, then ask your child to choose the best sentence for each picture.

Parents

46

He took his glasses off.

Funky Fox went surfing.

Reading directions

Tess is visiting her grandad.
Follow her directions to find how she got there.
Trace her route with your finger.

I go out of my house, past the post box, through the field of sheep, over the bridge, through the playground, across the zebra crossing, and into the block of flats. Grandad lives on the ground floor.

This activity will help your child to recognise that words are used as directions.

Read the directions with them, then ask them to draw which way Tess goes on the map.

Where do I start?

Nicholas is trying to read these words, but the sentences are back to front! Help him to sort them out. Write them in the correct order.

1. mum.
my love I

_____

_____

2. dad. my love I

_____

_____

This activity will help your child to learn that the order of words is important.

Read each sentence aloud first, to show that they don't yet make sense.

Parents

47

3. Fred. called is cat My

_____

_____

4. granny. my with school to go I

_____

_____

35

Shandy Shark

Read this story. Look for the words that begin with **sh**. Circle them, then write them in Shandy Shark.

Shandy Shark lived in the sea. When she saw the other fish, she showed all her teeth and made them swim away.

Everyone was scared of Shandy Shark. "I wish someone would be my friend," said Shandy.

She saw a little shellfish. "Will you be my friend?" she said. "Sure!" said the shellfish. "Shall we go for a swim?"

Shandy and the shellfish swam to the top of the sea to look at all the ships sailing by.

"Ship ahoy!" they shouted, then dived back down to the seabed for shelter.

This activity will help your child to recognise and read 'sh' words.

Ask them to circle the 'sh' words and write them inside Shandy Shark.

Charlie Chat

Read this story. Look for the words that begin with **ch**. Circle them, then write them in the speech bubble.

Charlie Chat loved to chat.
He liked to invite his friend
Chimpi Chimpanzee to chat
and share chocolate.

Chimpi Chimpanzee liked to
cook, so he always brought
chicken, cheese, pork chops and
chips to eat. Charlie made some
hot chocolate to drink, too.

"Chat, chat, chat," went Charlie
and Chimp as they ate the food.
They loved the chat and
chocolate party.

Thumper the Kangaroo

Read this story. Look for the words that begin with **th**. Circle them and write them in the thought bubble.

Thumper loved to thump. Thursday was his favourite thumping day. He hopped around thumping all the other animals with his paws.

"Ow!" they said. "Stop that! Thump your tail on the ground, not us!"

"That is a great idea," said Thumper, so he thumped his tail, thump, thump, thump.

"Thank you," said Thumper, and he thumped his way to the end of Thursday.

▶ This activity will help your child to recognise and read 'th' words.

▶ Remind them to use capital letters where appropriate.

Parents

47

thump thump

41

Further activities

4–5

► You can repeat this 'Match the words' activity with any list of words that your child is using often, for instance, 'mum', 'dad', 'my', 'like', 'look', 'went', 'want'. When you write out the list, make sure each word and letter can be seen clearly.

► Extend further by making a 'Snap!' game of words. To do this, write out two lists of the same words on a piece of card, and cut each word out. Mix up the words, and share them out amongst the players. Then use them to play 'Snap!'. The winner is the player who is left with most words at the end of the game.

► You can use this game as a way to introduce new words, too.

6–7

► Write each word from this page on a piece of card, and play a game. Lay the cards in a pile in the middle of the table and take it in turns to pick up one card at a time. If each player can read the word on the card, they get to keep it. The winner is the player who has most word cards at the end of the game.

► Gradually add new words to the game as your child becomes a more confident reader.

► Extend the idea by writing full sentences on the game cards from familiar story books which your child is able to read.

8–9

► Ask your child to write about their own experiences in the same way as the activity, for example, 'I am at home', 'I am with my mum'. If they can't write the whole sentence, write most of it for them, then ask them to read it, and write in the missing word. The word should be 'I', 'we' or 'you'.

► *Answers: 1. We, 2. I, 3. You, 4. I, 5. You.*

-11

▶ Make a list of verbs such as 'hop', 'laugh' and 'giggle', which your child can then use to make up their own two-word sentences, for example, 'he plays', 'she jumps', so they can learn the spellings. This will help them to write independently.

▶ Then write some sentences, ask your child to read them and draw a picture to go with each one.

▶ To broaden their learning, introduce the word 'they'.

▶ *Answers: 1. He, 2. He, 3. She, 4. He, 5. She, 6. She,*

-13

▶ Children find it difficult to move from statements to asking simple questions, so this activity will help them learn how to do it.

▶ Write some other questions with 'yes/no' answers, such as 'Do sharks fly?' 'Do trees run?' for your child to read and reply to.

▶ Ask them to write simple questions like this which have a 'yes' or 'no' answer.

▶ *Answers: 1. Yes 2. Yes 3. No 4. Yes 5. No 6. No*

-15

▶ Make a picture and word 'Snap!' game to play with your child.

▶ Draw a picture on one piece of card and the word describing it on another, and repeat for several different words – for ideas of which

words to include, look in a familiar story or reference book. Share the cards out between the players, and play in the same way as 'Snap!'. The player to say 'Snap!' first, when a word matches a picture, gets to keep both cards. The winner is the player with the most cards at the end of the game.

▶ Introduce new words to the game regularly so that your child learns to recognise them.

▶ *Answers: 1. Teddy bear 2. Train 3. Book 4. Umbrella 5. Ball 6. Duck 7. Car 8. Computer 9. Scissors*

Further activities

16-17

▶ Ask your child to write about where else Abdul would go in the park, using the same sentence structure, for example, 'Sam is going to the tree'.

▶ Ask them to write about where they are going, for example, 'I am going to school'. A simple picture dictionary will help with ideas, and with the spelling of the nouns at the end of each sentence. Always encourage your child to read back anything they have written.

▶ *Answers: 1. Abdul is going to the park. 2. Abdul is going to the swings. 3. Abdul is going to the ice cream van. 4. Abdul is going to the pond.*

18-19

▶ Ask your child to write your shopping list, to read it and tick things off as you go round the supermarket. If they want to find out how to spell words to make a list, give them a simple word and picture dictionary, or look at labels on the food in the cupboards at home. Ask them to make other lists, too – things to take on holiday or to school, things to do this week.

▶ Give your child the opportunity to write other lists independently, too.

▶ Ask them to read the list back later as well, to make sure they can recall what they have written.

▶ *Answers: The lists will vary.*

20-21

▶ Look for other recipes which you can make together. Point out how they are written, for example, a list of ingredients followed by a list of instructions.

▶ Write a simple recipe together – how to make a sandwich, for example – with you doing the writing. This will provide a model for your child to then have a go at writing a recipe on their own.

▶ Ask them to read back their recipe, to check it makes sense. They may spell some words wrongly. If it contains words they should know how to spell, such as 'the', 'in' or 'on', say something like 'I heard you read that word, but I can't see it. Can you write it in for me?'.

- Ask your child to write an answer to Jill's letter, and to make sure it answers her question.
- Ask them why the letter reads 'Love from Jill x' at the end.
- Let them read some of your letters to find out how they can finish a letter, and make sure they know why they need to write their own name at the end. This will prepare them for more complex letter writing later on.
- Read some envelopes together so they can see what to write, then make some envelopes, and write some letters to friends.

- Repetition of words and writing is an extremely valuable exercise for children.
- Ask your child to carry on the story substituting new animal names.
- Read other stories with your child which use repetitive language. This will enable your child to predict words more easily, and so to gain confidence to read independently.
- Ask them to write similar stories on their own and to reread them, checking that they make sense.
- *Answers: 1. In goes the cat. Splish, splash. 2. In goes*

the duck. Splish, splash. 3. In goes the dog. Splish, splash. 4. In goes the pig. Splish, splash.

- This activity will help your child become familiar with 'the', 'and', 'they', 'cat' and 'dog' . When you read the text with your child, make sure they read from left to right, and that they understand the relationship between the written and spoken word.

- To extend the idea, ask your child to make up their own version substituting family names for each character, or to change the story using the same characters to push a car out of a ditch.
- You can write the story with your child. They should then be able to read it back independently.
- *Answers: 2. Dog. 3. Dog, Frog. 4. Dog, Frog, Cat. 5. Frog, Rat.*

Further activities

28-29

▶ Ask your child to find as many things in the picture that rhyme, then to draw their own ideas onto the picture to show more rhyming objects.

▶ Ask them think of real or nonsense words that rhyme, for example 'pig', 'tig', 'wig', 'fig', 'big', 'lig', so that they really understand rhyme. Encourage them to write a sentence using two or three rhyming words that you give them, such as 'goat', 'boat', 'float'.

▶ *Answers: The words that rhyme on this page are sheep, peep, steep; dog, log, frog; pig, wig; goat, boat; boy, Roy toy; man, Stan; house, mouse; well, bell.*

30-31

▶ Develop this idea by writing four sentences to go with four pictures. Ask your child to cut out and glue each sentence underneath the appropriate picture. This will give them the opportunity to read sentences independently, after writing them with you, which will give them more confidence with reading.

▶ Write three or four sentences about a story your child has just read. Cut them out, jumble them up, and ask your child to sort them out into order, first, second, third, fourth. Do this with individual letters in new words, too.

32-33

▶ Ask your child to use the map to say directions for the way granddad would go to get to Tess's house. You can write the directions down, or they can, then ask your child to read them to make sure they make sense.

▶ Ask them to give you directions to a relative or a friend's house, and when you go there next, introduce the terms left and right. Ask them to draw a map showing the way, with arrows and labels marking clearly what they pass on the way.

▶ To extend further, look at how words are used for other purposes – newspapers, adverts and signs, for example.

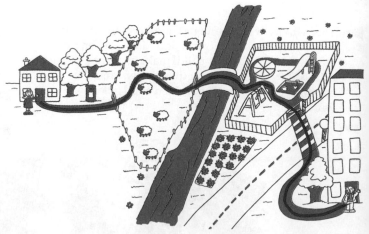

Whenever your child reads any text, make sure they start at the top and on the left-hand side of the page, and that they do the same with independent writing.

▶ Broaden the activity by writing more sentences back to front for your child to sort out. Keep them simple to start with, using words that are already familiar. Then ask your child to sort out a sentence in which two or three words are put in the wrong place, for example, 'My cat fish. eats'

▶ *Answers: 1. I love my mum. 2. I love my dad. 3. My cat is called Fred. 4. I go to school with my granny.*

▶ With your child, use a picture dictionary to look up more words that begin with 'sh'. Write a list of words that end with the 'sh' sound, for example, 'fish', 'wish', 'crash', 'bash'.

▶ Ask your child to write a sh story, and give them a title and a list of words to start them off, such as Shelby and the shark.

Answers: Shandy, Shark, she, showed, shellfish, shall, ship, ships, shouted, shelter.

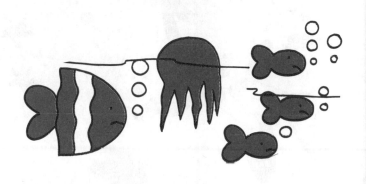

ask your child to look for words that end with 'ch', such as 'church' and 'much'.

▶ Write a list of 'ch' words together, asking your child to write the 'ch' part at the beginning or the end, with you writing the rest of each word.

▶ *Answers: Charlie, Chat, chat, Chimpi, Chimpanzee, chocolate, chicken, cheese, chops, chips.*

▶ Look for other words that start with a 'ch' sound in a picture dictionary and in your child's favourite books, like 'cheep', 'chair', 'chin'. Then

▶ Ask your child to look for other 'th' words when they are reading a story, either words that begin with 'th' or words that end with 'th'.

▶ Ask them to count how many 'th' words are on one page or, if it is a short story, how many 'th' words there are in the book.

▶ Extend this further by asking them to write more about Thumper the Kangaroo. Let them talk about their ideas first and write a list of 'th' words they could use in their story.

▶ *Answers: Thumper, thump, Thursday, thumping, the, they, that, thumped, thank.*

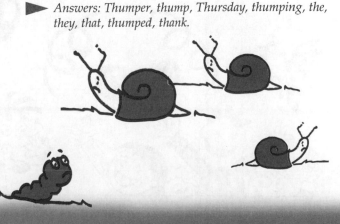

Celebration!

You are so clever! Colour the stars to show what you know!

I can read ten new words.

I can read a nursery rhyme.

I can read a recipe.

I can read a story.